Self-Portrait as Wikipedia Entry

Self-Portrait as Wikipedia Entry

DEAN RADER

COPPER CANYON PRESS

Port Townsend, Washington

Cover art: Marnie Spencer, *Portrait of a Poet* (2006), 7⅛" × 9¼", acrylic on canvas.

Copper Canyon Press is in residence at Fort Worden State Park in Port Townsend, Washington, under the auspices of Centrum. Centrum is a gathering place for artists and creative thinkers from around the world, students of all ages and backgrounds, and audiences seeking extraordinary cultural enrichment.

LIBRARY OF CONGRESS CATALOGING-IN-PUBLICATION DATA

Names: Rader, Dean, author.
Title: Self-portrait as Wikipedia entry / Dean Rader.
Description: Port Townsend, Washington : Copper Canyon Press, [2017]
Identifiers: LCCN 2016014770 | ISBN 9781556595080 (pb : alk. paper)
Subjects: | BISAC: POETRY / American / General. | LITERARY COLLECTIONS /
   American / General.
Classification: LCC PS3618.A3476 A6 2016 | DDC 811/.6--dc23
LC record available at https://lccn.loc.gov/2016014770

9 8 7 6 5 4 3 2 FIRST PRINTING

COPPER CANYON PRESS
Post Office Box 271
Port Townsend, Washington 98368

www.coppercanyonpress.org

FOR MY FAMILY

Being inclines intrinsically to self-concealment.
HERACLITUS

Not only is the self entwined in society; it owes society its existence in the most literal sense.
THEODOR ADORNO

The Nation has not yet found peace from its sins.
W.E.B. DU BOIS

A line is a dot that went for a walk.
PAUL KLEE (ACCORDING TO WIKIPEDIA)

Contents

Self-Portrait as Wikipedia Entry

Self-Portrait with Reader

I want to begin by letting you know
that the title is no lie, even though
this poem is not quite a portrait of
reader and writer. It's really a love

letter to the not-yet-known from the soon-
to-be-forgotten, which the author is
supposed to be, like stars on a warm June
day. But what I need to tell you is this:

wherever you are, turn to the person
sitting next to you—whether you are on
a bus, in class, in a car, in heaven—

and say, *Lovely Stranger, you appear in*
the last lines of a poem written to
the good and grave world. Now, what will you do?

Give me the sheriff star pinned to the mermaid
and that tiny piece of wood from your throat.
Give me the saw blade, the plastic cat's-eye.
Give me the flash drive of your tongue:

I want to save everything. Even the goat horns
you strapped to the skull of the little girl,
and yes, both of her hands. No, I don't really
know what that means, but so what?

I'll take the boneyard and all its yellow flowers,
I'll take the pisspot, the necklace of petal fire,
and while I'm at it, I'll take the body's wafer:
I'll take whatever breaks down beneath its own sad weight—

whether it's this life or a bad party. Your tangy
pelt, your twitch. You want my sandwich,
hey, get in line. This isn't the army, but I'll march.
I want your shoulder holster, I want your mouth of bullets.

Apocryphal Self-Portrait

The coldest winter I ever saw was the summer I spent in San Francisco.
ATTRIBUTED TO MARK TWAIN, BUT ITS ORIGINS ARE UNKNOWN

The darkest night of my life was that morning in your car. My heart
would not stop storming. You said it was climate change. I may not

be able to prove you wrong, but that doesn't mean the end is near.
The end is always near. I read somewhere that the sum of the earth's water

will never change. Nothing is taken away, nothing added. Every
drop is the same age, every age dyed in the same drop. The

cut-up clouds stretched and strung out have had about enough.
Each day is a boat on a lake that we row ourselves into. We try

to pick at the scab of sunlight itching overhead, but we can't take
our eye off the little crack in the hull we know keeps growing.

The Buddha says every place we've been we stay. Right now, he's
in my dream sitting alone at an empty table, my tiny chair about

to collapse beneath him. Mark Twain walks into the room looking
exactly like Colonel Sanders. In one hand, he cradles a bucket

of chicken, in the other he carries an ax. *The heaviest weight is the
lightness of the soul*, he says to the Buddha. *Give in to the dark,*

the Buddha replies, *and you won't feel the darkness.* The longest
drive we ever took was that evening we parked next to the cliff.

The sidereal dashboard, the cracked windshield of the body. I want you to know that it is never the darkest right before the dawn.

I want you to know the truth about everything. I want you to know that when those memories drop down, my umbrella opens.

Cartography;
or American Allegory I

after Bruce Snider

Once upon a time in Oklahoma,
there was no such thing as Oklahoma.

When I look out off the coast of California,
I am standing on our farm in Hinton, Oklahoma.

Answer: Because Texas sucks and Kansas blows.
Question: Why is it so windy in Oklahoma?

All roads might lead to Rome,
but all trails take you to Oklahoma.

The stars dragged along in their wagons of dust,
the moon on its cot, the last long light of Oklahoma.

Pawhuska, Nuyaka, Wewoka, Taloga, Oologah,
Okemah, Eufaula. O, the missing maps of Oklahoma.

Knife wind, ice wind, blind wind, hatchet wind, stone wind,
skin wind, dust wind, and must wind all whisper *Oklahoma.*

I think of Bruce Snider floating above the corn of Indiana.
Is he waving at Jesus rising above the wheat of Oklahoma?

I have often wondered if there is more oil
or blood beneath the soil of Tulsa, Oklahoma.

My second baptism was in the First Baptist Church.
My first was in the summer rains of Oklahoma.

State amphibian: bullfrog. State beverage: milk. State soil:
Port Silt Loam. State mammal: bison. State song: "Oklahoma."

The first dead body I saw was my friend Kevin Wright's.
I was six years old in a funeral home in Weatherford, Oklahoma.

It's time to talk about the scent of Denise Barker's cautious
skin. It was like mist on a summer sidewalk in Oklahoma.

Recently uncovered manuscript from Ovid in
which the gods learn to play football in Oklahoma.

Where are you, Rhonda Harder, first girl to kiss me?
I'm sorry your name became a joke for the boys of Oklahoma.

Put down your pen, Lord Death. The names of
my parents are not yet on your list for Oklahoma.

If you ask me what one is to do with this world,
I will tell you that the answer is not to be found in Oklahoma.

Poem of the open prairie, couplet of the spread-out sky,
metaphor of mistletoe and milkweed: who will write Oklahoma?

God has bequeathed himself to the grape leaves of Sonoma
and the fog of San Francisco. Is his next gift to Oklahoma?

My grandfather and my son share the name Dean Rader. This morning my
son sinks into our bright bed, my grandfather into the dark dirt of Oklahoma.

Frog Considers a Photograph by Andres Serrano Entitled *Dissection*

I don't know what this is, Frog says to Toad, who is at the stove
stirring pea soup the same color as Frog's skin. Toad is thinking

about beauty, which, he has just decided, is an empty bowl
a second or two before the first drops of green. *Everything,*

Toad says to the wooden spoon, *is about anticipation.* He glances
at Frog who has turned the book of photographs upside down

to get, it appears, a different angle. He is still looking at the
same photo. Beauty, thinks Toad, is the opposite of scrutiny.

He wants Frog to put down the book and come join him,
but Frog lets out a little groan before leaning over to rest his head

against the open pages. The book lies flat on the coffee table,
Frog's face lies flat on the pages of the book. Toad cannot see

the photo, but it seems to be something lying flat on a table.
Toad watches Frog rise up and stare at the wall for several seconds,

maybe a minute, his huge eyes as round and smooth as two glass balls.
Frog knows dinner will be ready soon, but wonders if he will ever be able

to eat again or look in a mirror or listen to music or go to a doctor
or think about art. Toad likes to play a little game at this time every evening:

he imagines what Frog is thinking before he gets up from the sofa
and comes to the table. He often assumes Frog is singing to himself

and tries to guess the song: "Lemon Tree." "Rainin' in My Heart." "Colinda."
"Joy to the World." But today he knows Frog is not singing. He knows

Frog is ready for pea soup. In fact, he seems to be meditating
in preparation for dinner, perhaps even praying. Toad is so moved

he begins to sing himself and has decided to give Frog extra soup
because Frog's reverie is one of expectation. Frog gets up, turns to

look once more at the photograph. The book begins, he believes,
to float. His eyes won't focus. The word *scalpel* begins to go deep

inside him. He looks over at Toad, who is cradling a pot of soup.
Frog has never seen Toad's smile so big, and the space

between them is suddenly like something sliced open,
each of them waiting to see what comes next.

Etiological Self-Portrait

Not with a bang but a baby's breath
not with a scream but a scratch
not with the angel but its after-ash
not with the dead but with their dreams:

we all want to rise up into that which
we have only now begun to know—
time might be a cup of tea
or a hummingbird above the rosebush—

we can never be sure, just like now,
after a day of fog and heavy gray
we wonder about the sun in its little barrow
of light and who might be pushing it.

The Poem Chooses Its Own Adventure

And now the poem is on a bus somewhere in
Marrakech scratching its way along one of
the old roads south of the Djemaa el-Fna. No
one recognizes it of course. The poem
is unshaven, sandaled, and wearing a poncho.
On its head a maroon fez. Who knows the last time
the poem bathed; it could be weeks. The poem smells
like your ass. If you want the poem to smell like
something else, you have to skip down seven lines.
You would not have chosen Morocco for the poem.
You hate sardine balls, and you're convinced people
only eat couscous because it sounds funny. The poem
is tired of you. It needed to get away. You ask so much
of it these days. Your demands are extravagant. You
wanted the poem to take you to Paris. You entertained
fantasies of coffee and croissants. You had even
spoken to your friends of *élan* and *joie de vivre*. When was the
last time you did anything for the poem? It's always about
you, still is, you know. Even now in line 19, you can't
get past your own expectations. But the poem has needs of
its own. It's like a dog that was born on a leash. It's like
a dog. It's like a leash. Snap it on. Tell it to bark. Tell it to lie
down. Make it beg. You've forced it to sleep outside its whole
life, and now it's in a jungle in Bolivia, an ashram in Odisha, a
whorehouse in Amsterdam. You didn't even know you
wanted a poem with the word *whorehouse* in it, but the
poem did. And that's the difference. It's about *care*. It's
about *attention*. It's about giving, and let's face it: you are
a taker. And so the poem is golfing in Orlando, hiking in
the Alps. If you want a poem that *inspires* you, that *rocks your world,*
you have chosen the wrong poem. The poem has had it

with you. It's rolling a joint for Ginsberg, it's digging its
way out of the Dust Bowl, it's fighting for the Confederates,
it's helping Geronimo shoot a white man, it's killed Lewis
and is seducing Clark's wife. The poem picks evasion, it
selects erasure, it opts for abandonment. It wants you out
of its life. It's decided it was wrong about *beauty*. And though
it might be indifferent to *love,* it's coming back for *glory.* And
now the poem is in the backseat of a cab, your address in
the GPS. Its sideburns are longer, it's wearing a dress, its fur
glistens in the blue lights of the dashboard. It's on all fours.
You are fast asleep in front of the television. And now
it's line 43, and the poem is tired of playing games,
and so it has finally decided, despite everything
you might have expected, to end it all right here.

Self-Portrait with Obfuscation

The trees turn
in the evening air

from black to blacker
even though the moon's

tiny headlamp lumbers
along through the dark

shaft of the sky's deep
mine. Twilight, strangely

dull, climbs into its
train and chugs back

to the surface where
everything goes on

as before. How does
something acquire

luminous meaning?
How does anything

not happen? What men
in another age called

revelation is blurring
at the edges. Nothing

is clearer than that
which obstructs us.

I'm tired of description
the way I'm tired of

possibility. I want
the light on the other

side of the light.
I want the dark

the darkness darkens.

Self-Portrait with Contemplation

In the "First Duino Elegy," my student writes,
Rilke uses form to convey meaning, and I think

about what it means to form, what it
means to convey, what it means to mean,

and I think of Rilke, alone, wandering along
the cliffs of the Adriatic, blind to his want.

There is something about the autumn
evening. Something about the air in

the evening in autumn. He is thin,
his beard not yet gray; his coat stiff

as the robe of a dead saint. Sometimes
our prayer is only for silence.

God and all angels sing the world to sleep,
the terrifying night a blank note

in the blackness. One day we might
endure that call which shapes itself

out of sorrow. *Come,* we say to the voice,
there is nothing you can tell us

we don't already know. What is ours
we have already given away, and what

belongs to the world we can never
truly own, including our own lives.

Who is to say we are not more
at home on the other side of death

where no border exists between you
and the angelic? The closer you are

the easier it is to hear.
Proximity is not only for lovers.

It is evening, and there is something in
the air, something less like the wind

and more like a song. The air is in the wind,
and the wind is in the voice, and the angel

is deep in his arms. What is terror
but the disappearance of beauty?

Everything we do, I write in the margin
of her essay, *"conveys" meaning.*

The poem needs form to convey, to carry,
to transport, to move across.

Down here. Down here.
Humbler. Lower.

I think of him and the blank sheaves
of the dead. I think of God as a breath

in the ear of the deaf. I think of
our voice as a cathedral for God's

mouth. Prayer, I hear you the way
God hears the future he has yet

to form into a word. God, I think
of the way you use form to deliver.

It is evening. I think of Rilke and the
longing for infinity and absence

rung into the deep stillness of the self.
If silence is bitter, change yourself to song.

O listener, I think of you alone there
on the cliff's edge of your daily duties,

waiting, the way saints wait, for the
falling to cease and the fire to rise,

when the tiniest note, the loveliest letter
from this world finally arrives.

Twenty Lines on Paul Klee's *The Man in Love*

In each stanza of this poem
There are five lines
One for the first time
I put my finger
On your bottom lip

One for the night
You slept next to me
For eight straight hours
Another for the next life
In which you'll kill me

One more for
Sorrow's tiny knot
You may one day
Untie
And one last one

For that slice of sky
The heavy leaf the cupped
Hand the opened lip in
And into which we fall
Without belt or net

Poem of Prevarication to Begin the Second Section

In the beginning, there was the latticework of the body.
You climbed me the way a cat . . .

     wait, let me start over.

In the latticework of the body, we began.
You climbed inside me. Fixed there like an
eye in a socket. You saw everything:
     nooks of desire,
          my tiny bones of snow.

[or:]

you broke my nooks of desire,
          my tin bones of now.

     [let's start here]

In the beginning was the empty
square of the heart. Marked with an *X*.

I need to rephrase that. It was more like:

          the beginning was little more
             than an empty square.
     There was no heart in the body.
          There was no body.

     [the reader may prefer this]

There was no beginning. There was
only the work of the heart. There was
only the heart.

In the everything of desire,
there is only work. There is no heart
only the inside of *X*.

O heart, O *X*, O snowy body of desire,
O lost reader—
Only you believe in beginnings:

Poem in Which Readers Select Their Favorite Title

A) Study on the Distance but Inevitability of War
B) Still Life with Manifest Destiny
C) Sesshu Toyo: A Homage
D) Depressed by the Programming Options on Fox, I Stumble
   Outside into a Cloudless Night
E) American Landscape

Somewhere the stars
have clicked on their little lamps
and gone hunting.

Only in darkness can you see
the light.
           Only by drowning
do you learn to swim.

Nothing is harder to believe in
than belief, and yet here
we are,
        at it again,

never really knowing
if we are the arrow
or the bow.
             The moon

unwinds its scarf
and dives into the pond.
Nothing on the water

but the strange shadows
of this life.
        I could
walk over to the edge

to look for whatever
I have lost,
but instead I'll lean

my grief against
two or three pines
        and walk away.

Self-Portrait Bop

after Langston Hughes

If it hasn't killed you by now
Just wait. This doesn't mean you
Can fly. In the quarter, in the
Shadows. The supermarket sea,
A blue safari, a pot of collard greens,
A field of flower seeds. These are things

America never was. America to me

Is what it isn't, like a missing comma
Or the lost digit. A hat with no head.
It is neither the water nor the wine.
No ax, no hammer, no chain. No
Ribbon, no box. White sheets but no bed.
Life never was life, but then again,

America never was America. To me,

To you, to the darkness. To him,
To her, to the blackest. O treble clef,
O bass note. Who is not
Both the music and the breath?
Both the letters and the page? Men might
Make a country, but what I wrote about

America was never America to me.

American Self-Portrait II: Study of the Other Self

Distance and inward, light and
the reversal of light, retread
tread and footfall. So much and so long,
the little voice within the little voice
says.
      We all
hide somewhere, why not in ourselves?

Existence is nothing more
                        than experience divided by endurance.

Think of me as the broken you—
the part of you you know needs
more than a splint and a bandage.
I am the fracture,
                the busted bone you refuse to lose.

I am that rhyme [there even when
I'm not], and you are the
intake after rhyme:
                silence, echo, wave in
the wave of waves.

If sorrow were a cup of pudding,
if sorrow were the spike of light
on the little pond, if sorrow were the pond
and you were the spike of waves,
                  the little light in the silent rhyme.

If life were a sling, it would
still break your arm. If your arm
were forgiveness, I'd break it again.

Believe me when I tell you
that there is nothing beyond
these words, that wall, your name—

here, stick your arm through the bar,
I want to sign your cast.

Relational Self-Portrait

The universe has not been built to scale—
everything is bigger or smaller than
it seems: the sea, the hole, a ship, a sail,

your line, the hook, your heart—that's where the nail
of desire drives deep. Sorrow can span
a universe that is not built to scale

even though rungs are strung from star to shell
and back. We end of course where we began
(that ship, that hole, that sea). And so we sail

full speed toward the iceberg—too fast to tell
if size or scale or course is plot or plan.
The universe will not be built to scale.

The dead in heaven, the living in hell,
blaze and burn in the blue of all that can
rise and fall. The ship of this life will sail

until its stern snaps beneath the stretched swell
at the end of the end. We find out then
the universe has not been built to scale
and that our want expands like wind not sail.

Labor;
or American Allegory II

I am fifteen. It is the summer
        of 1982. I'm working illegally
at the Sonic Drive-In,
        Weatherford, Oklahoma.

I am a carhop, and as such,
        I am required to wear
a Sonic baseball hat, the front
        two quadrants of which are

made of some sort of soft
        foam. The rest of the hat is mesh.
The hat's bill feels squishy
        like the Tater Tots I carry

to the car in bay 3, a tow truck
        to be precise. I see as I
reach out to hook the
        tray onto the driver's

window that the woman
        in the passenger seat is
crying into a knot of Kleenex.
        She is also wearing

a hat, the one mandated for
        all employees at our local
McDonald's franchise. She works
        the drive-through. I am thinking

many things as the driver,
        a man I do not know, mines
his pockets, the glove compartment,
        the space between the vinyl seats,

for the amount needed to pay
        for the Tater Tots, the cherry
limeade, and the Vanilla Coke.
        My memory is $1.72. I think

of a boy my age in someplace
        I can only think of, a place
like India or Colombia, and what
        he would have to do

in his country to earn $1.72 in 1982.
        The man does not have
enough money to pay for the food
        and drinks, and he asks if I

can take the Coke back, We'll share
        the limeade, he says to the boy
holding the tray and to the girl
        still weeping, the hat flat in her lap.

In 1982, if a person were to
        start his car, back out of the bay
at the Sonic, make a left onto
        Main Street and head west

to the nearby on-ramp of Interstate 40,
        he might get on the highway
and drive west toward Elk City, Sayre, Erick,
        and look out his window, and in

any direction, he might see as many
        as thirty oil rigs at one time.
He might wonder about the men,
        where they are on their fourteen-hour

shift, the hard paste on their skin,
        the enormous greased chain
whipping around the dark shaft of the drill.
        That man might wonder about

drilling, about the future of fuel, about
        the cost of the gas in his tank,
about how oil becomes petroleum and so
        he will not consider the young man

from Watonga whose left foot was crushed
        in the early dawn when the drill bit slipped
off the coupler as it emerged from
        the hole in the ground nearly one hundred times

the length of his truck. He will not think
        of the crew chief, the ambulance driver,
the ER doctor, the scrambling screaming
        roughnecks, the truckers charging past,

the highway patrolmen arriving at the scene,
        or their fathers who poured the asphalt
for the highway thirty years before, or
        the men who will haul the heavy barrels

of sludge, the farmer who sold his land
        to the oil company, the backhoe driver who dug
the first hole, the paramedic in the back of
        the ambulance unsure of what she'll see.

The driver will not think of
        the man at the wheel of the tow
truck who was called to the scene
        of an accident at an oil rig to haul

the victim's car back to town. He will not
        think of the girl who took an extra job mopping
the floors of the Weatherford General Hospital
        one morning a week to make extra

money for her college fund or what
        she said when she saw her brother
who should be at work hurried
        into the emergency room, his

Wranglers sliced up the side and his
        entire leg wrapped in red rags
or what her father said to her in bay 3
        of the Sonic Drive-In as he described what

it was like to arrive at a rig accident
        to do his job. And the driver will certainly
not think of the boy at the Sonic violating
        the Fair Labor Standards Act in the summer

of 1982 or what this boy will remember
        at his desk thirty-two years later, lost
in an impossible task that almost
        no one would consider work.

Frog and Toad Confront Bashō beneath the Wreckage of the Moon

Toad leaps from the stone
into the river's black heart.
Frog pictures the stone.

Beneath the stars, there
is only a frog, a toad,
the reader, the stars.

A fisherman in
a boat. A line still in the
water. A whole life.

Old pond, old water,
old poem, old sound, old frog,
old toad, old splash, old.

Don't imitate Frog—
leaves do not mimic the wind
nor the wind Toad's breath.

Snow on the mountain,
water in the pond, Toad and
Frog leap in the moon.

))

A man's heart? An owl
asleep in the branches? Which
one hears death step first?

))

This summer night in
this dark pond—absolutely
no one is swimming.

))

Everything is in
motion: gods, like frogs, refuse
to stay in one place.

))

A lily pad sinks,
and a lily pad rises:
a new world is born.

))

The river is move-
ing. The blackbird must be fly-
ing. The toad? Eat-ing?

))

A pail of water.
A woodpile and an ax.
A toad and a frog.

))

In the deepest pool,
and in the darkest water,
there swims a tadpole.

))

Morning on its long
journey, wind in the grasses,
the frog wakes the toad.

Autumnal Self-Portrait

with a line by Cole Swensen

If a garden is the world counted,
a dozen flowers in the sky might
be the heart of Jesus on fire
                    or the blue flame of nothing.

Nothing is always added to something,
                            or so say the mathematicians.
Nothing is what the world owes you,
                        or so says my father.

The wind hitches up its trailer,
                    drags its load once more into darkness.

Things are about to start and to end.

Every second of every day in this world
a leaf divides itself,
                    an endless remainder of the undone.

Not even God knows how many have fallen.

Our days are less a series than a sequence,
                            our nights more formula than function.
We've become used to everything by now,
                        except our own lives,
those perennials we lose only once.

The trees have started their quiet calculations.
The stiff sun turns away from the dieback and shuffles on.

The moon has a clock deep in its throat.
It ticks its way back to the first morning,

                            where it subtracts loss from loss,
where it adds the given to the made,

                      divides the distance,
        mitigates the abandoned.

Season of threshold, I want to wear you on the inside.

This is the time of year when the world learns
to wear its light.

             I want to rise up out of the field to receive it.

A Page of Spring

Paul Klee, *Ad Marginem* (1930)

I

The sea's sky tides out
to lichen light and a stuck sun.
Night coils back and slurs.

Dawn tears into the weather, or
is it the weather that rips into fogshine:
the clouds' flicked votives
and the leaves little wicks ignite.

II

Once upon
a time
there was
no time
only
the page.

III

Plants absorb light primarily using the pigment chlorophyll.
Cellular respiration allows for the conversion of light energy

to chemical energy. Palisade mesophyll. Stem and infiltration
of stem. Terra and terawatt. Light begets the absence of light.

IV

Once upon a page
there was no horizon,
only inversion.

In a world of margin, there is no margin.
Within the border there is no border.

We've moved on from the first idea,
never more acute than in its vanishing.

V

Spindlestem, ropestem, ladlestem.
Heaven is always in the margin,
but in what direction?

VI

The parts of a typical leaf include the upper

and lower epidermis, the mesophyll, the vascular

bundle(s) (veins), and the stoma(ta).

VII

Parchment of leaf-life, parched sugar sun,
wind up and convert our lost letters,

turn light into light, make our eyes
see the eye in sea and leaf light.

Crown of thistle thorn, we wear you
the way the sun wears the cross

we've nailed it to. The vascular
bundle, God's other stoma,

never bleeds out.

VIII

You are upside down, not the bird.

Alternate Self-Portrait

One day

I will drift

into darkness

and know it

perhaps

the way a son

recognizes a mother

after he has returned

from many years

of travel

understanding

the new distance

is neither

beginning nor

ending

only stillness

America, I Do Not Call Your Name without Hope

after Neruda

America, I do not call your name without hope
not even when you lay your knife
against my throat or lace my hands
behind my back, the cuffs connecting
us like two outlaws trying to escape
history's white horse, its heavy whip
a pistolshot in the ear. Lost land,
this is a song for the scars on your back,
for your blistered feet and beautiful
watch, it is for your windmills, your
magic machines, for your fists. It
is for your wagon of blood, for your dogs
and their teeth of fire, for your sons
and the smoke in their hearts. This is for
your verbs, your long lurk, your whir.
This is for you and your fear, your tar,
for the white heat in your skin, and
for your blue bones that one day may sing.
This is for your singing. This is for the past,
but not for what's passed. This is for daybreak
and backbreak, for dreams, and for darkness.
This song is not for your fight but it is a song
for fighting. It is a song of flame but not for burning.
It is a song out of breath but a plea for breathing.
It is the song I will sing when you knock
on my door, my son's name in your mouth.

Want;
or American Allegory III

Hieronymus Bosch, *The Haywain Triptych* (1516)

Dear Mr. Bosch,

I have been watching a homeless man stuff straw
        into the legs of his pants
we are in a park near a haystack he stands
        over the stack staring long
into the absence of what he has removed
        like a sculptor might gaze at
a block of granite after the excess is cut
        away I think Mr. Bosch
of the beggar on the front panels of *The*
        Haywain his stretched stick stopping
just above a scab of scattered bones as if
        he could wave it and make the
animal whole again but a black bird and
        a hungry dog want things to
stay as they are of course inside the painting
        the wagon has also stilled
as dozens of people grab at the hay with hands
        and hooks despite the fact that
lovers and angels sit atop the hay and
        the wagon is pulled by a
band of beasts and everyone perhaps even
        Jesus in the cloud above
wants what is taken away this morning a
        report on poverty in
the United States said that there had never
        been more people considered

poor even though nothing ever really goes
        away Mr. Bosch not in
this life desire is not a dog at the
        door and hunger is no horse
asleep beneath the umbrella of heaven
        it will not wake Mr. Bosch
and walk backward into the reins history
        has held we all want to climb
up into something we cannot understand
        even the man with the hay
dank in his pants even the lord lofted high
        on his fortune of air an
alternative to and protection from the
        avarice of the sod-strewn
world which is to say Mr. Bosch that this life
        is no more than a basket
strapped to the back of a beggar but who am
        I Mr. Bosch to talk
about allegory want as you know is
        neither icon nor idea
but invention a landscape molded and
        made for the man the
unfortunate man drawn into it

How We Survive: A Triptych

I

This morning I went for a jog
along the ocean wearing a cape
of starlight. The sky hummed
like a laptop just booted up, and
the ocean, well, the ocean had
opened early, so it was ready, it
knew what it wanted, which was
to be taken in and cradled like
a baby who had slept through
the night for the first time, and
so I ran toward the darkness I
knew I would split open, my cape
a sail of sky-shimmer against the
waves. Every dog on the beach
slowed to a trot, Frisbees and
tennis balls found their rightful
arc the only time that day. Even
the gulls circled back around a
second time, hoping to pedal
the tiny bicycle of light as it
rose and fell behind me. *Hop
on,* I say to my fears, who have
been trailing me since before
I began, *let me carry you
everywhere you want to go.*

II

This afternoon I took a nap
wearing a costume that looks

just like me. Inside it I felt like
another person who happened
to know so many things about me,
like my preference for almonds over
cashews, how sometimes, when
I am in a strange room, I imagine
hopping from one piece of
furniture to the next, how often
I think about the time my
grandmother spanked me when
I was six, and what exactly my body
looks like to other people. Inside
me, it seems particularly bad that
I can tell you almost nothing
about the poverty line, and that I am
frequently unclear about the distinctions
between Hamas, al-Qaeda, al-Shabaab,
al-Fatah, and the Taliban, not to mention
the difference between mass and weight,
in part because I am feeling very heavy
right now, as though I have begun
sinking into myself the way one
falls into a deep sleep, both of my
selves dreaming that I will wake out of
the wrong body and walk uncovered
into the mistaken world, ill equipped
for anything except regret.

III

Tonight I made love to you wearing
a suit of armor. I kept saying *armor,*
armor, armor over and over until you
reached up and closed the face mask.
Inside the helmet my voice hummed

like an engine on a long car ride,
my words driving me far into the
two-lane road of your body's night.
I tell you this even though I know
how much you hate it when
I recount the recent past, a
voice-over telling us either what we
already know or what we want
to find out. But the world comes
to us in stories, and this is how I
narrate the scenes of this life, and how
you mark my version of the night
against what really happened. This
is the way I make sense of darkness
and regret, how I let you know it's
okay to lift the mask and let me out.
It's how we survive, how we keep
going, or, at the very least, how we
know we haven't stopped, despite
the dogs at our heels and the little
hook of death deep in our skin.

American Self-Portrait III;
or What the Poet Thinks of Instead of War

Take off
        your dress of flame: the whole
world is raining.

      We can say
we are more than a trickle
of sun, but what, really,
do we want of surrender
                  but supplication?
      Our lives
are language, our desires
apophatic, but not in that
order.
      We want what
language won't do, and we
ask only what we
are prepared to live.
             Period pause
and line loss, this is what
we're left with.
         You and
the imperiled present,
you and the glove box of
the body, you and memory's
ice cube:
        What's in the glass?
the poem queries. Walk, the
garden commands. Stop here,
the poem types. Language
like desire pays attention only

to syntax—everything else
is metaphor.
          Your skin,
for example,
           is the crocus sky I
fall into, your dress the silk song
in desire's ear, and
              (are you still
with me?) your hands
            the silver sun striking the match.

Not Long after Rich: A Study

The will to be modern is more modern than
the will to be   Existence is a locomotive

pushing through a brush fire
in the mountains lost somewhere

between emergence and arrival
Nothing is more indefinite than redefinition—

task and destruction—the still-unbegun work
of repair   The undefiled snow on the slope

in winter is not a poem   She had

to get down from the blocked
train, her moment-stricken eye, like her

tongue, aflame   She will dive once more into
the difficult world   It will not be simple It will

take all her thought   If you have burned once you
may still burn again   Raise it up there,

taste what has soared into the air
You have a brutal thing to do

Frost on Fire

A thing that melts can also burn: like a
Thicket of ice in the pond, the cold net
Of stars, even the hard white ax of the
Heart. A man can freeze without getting wet

Just as he can lose without being lost,
But winter finds everyone, even though
We spend our whole lives eluding it. Frost
Reminds us of what is to come—the snow,

The sky, the trees, the skin, the sleet, the sleep.
How often have I woken in fear, blind
In my unknowing? The woods are dark and deep,
Even in the day; still the mind will find

Its way into the light, into the bright
Thaw of this life, where we, both flake and flame,
Fire and fall through. Let sun daze, let night
Show day how to blaze, let death drop its name.

Self-Portrait in Five Rooms

Pablo Neruda's house at Isla Negra

1) You collected
everything,
which
I had not
believed
until I
walked
into the insect
room:
beetles,
butterflies,
bugs
from every
continent,
run through
with
the tiniest
of pins,
flagless poles
claiming
the creature
for some
lost poetic
state.
I imagined
them
breaking free
one
night,

a march,
of liberation,
reclaiming
the land
the way
an insurgency
unpins the
trapped
body of
its country.

2) I could
name
every writer
whose picture
hangs on the wall
leading to
your study.
Their identities
will be
our
little secret.
But,
I have to ask
you about
Baudelaire,
his photograph
the only one
on your desk.
Perhaps
you mistook him
for E.A. Poe.
They look
very much alike.

But, of course,
he is French,
and that
comb-over
makes him
look like a
man who,
like Poe,
might know
something
about how
flowers
might bloom
from a
cadaver.

3) In which room
did I first
think of
Whitman?
It was
in fact
among the
figureheads:
priests, sea animals,
and a dozen
near-naked
mermaids
dangling from
the ceiling
like the gods
of all puppets.
I wondered
how you

might react
if
one night,
while dusting
the burnished
shoulders
of Medusa,
Walt
somehow came
alive and
slipped behind you,
removed your stiff
sailor's cap
and
pressed
his
hot lips
to your neck.
And
what would
you do
if he ran
his mouth
down
your back,
his soft
dead-man's beard
brushing your
skin
like the silvered
plumes of
a quill,
his husky
voice

murmuring
in broken Spanish,
He ido
marcando
con cruces
de fuego
el atlas
blanco
de tu
cuerpo . . .

4) It was
in the bedroom
where I
imagined
Matilde.
What can I say?
You were
downstairs
with Walt,
and the nights
are cold in
Isla Negra.
It would go
like this:
I catch her
drowsy,
half-asleep,
and
I say
to her:
Soy su Pablito.
Maybe I would
write a line

from one of
my poems
on the
inside
of her
right thigh,
so that
when your inky
fingers
tracked the
hidden paths
of her body
the spoor
you found
would be
mine.
But
I doubt
it.

5) But it was
on the beach,
walking around
the fence, the
heavy rocks,
the unbuckled
sea
where I
realized that
everything
eventually
ends up in
your house:
our nautical dreams,

our dusty shoes,
the vast
killing world.
Even the
voice of
this poem
is
now
part of your
collection.

Frog Considers Slipping Toad Pop Rocks™

It was when Frog realized he wanted to make
the one he loved more than any other suffer,
and then laugh at his misfortune,
that he decided to slip Toad some Pop Rocks.

The inside of Toad's mouth is exceedingly wet,
and Frog believes the rocks would have an unusually
explosive effect. Best if Snail and the Turtle Brothers
could be there, but why complicate the simple?

Nothing is more intimate than deliberate
cruelty, nothing says *I know you* like knowing
weakness. What is affinity but the absence
of variance? Can the heart be so full it needs

to be empty? Is there a better way to show
devotion than to help someone burst from within?

Becoming Klee, Becoming Color

Instead of the endless exercise of
    the sketch, instead of the trace.

Instead of mimicking Manet from
    memory, instead of absinthe and

afterglow. Instead of the screaming skull.
    Instead of. Ask, he does, of tenor

and timbre, for the hand to unbutton
    color's blouse. Instead of blouse.

He finds he knows shapes the way the sea
    knows its waves: the thing it flows

in and out of. He sees crimson so clearly he
    becomes crimson, black with such

clarity he turns blind. Instead of image.
    Over and over he rides the color wheel

deep into his mind's night, hoping to arrive
    at the right shape. When he closes his

eyes he tries to want what the colors want:
    the agony of onyx, the sorrow of burlywood,

the obsessions of oxblood. Over and over he
    asks of the colors to find their form.

Instead of folding into augur. What the mind
    never stops seeing: sienna as square,

terre verte as rhombus, cyan circle as the viridian
    light of digon. The azure arbelos. As

though his own, he accepts triangle's sharp sin,
    he takes on the salvation of the little

oval. Instead of triquetra. Instead of annulus.
    Instead of plane or line, he requests

pattern, but structures hide behind the colors
    that are not theirs. Harder than

lifting the waves from the seas themselves.
    He sees the seas so clearly, but

is neither ocean nor its waves.
    Not even red becomes red.

Of the form it must figure, the body asks.
    Let coral cylinder be the angel's

rib cage, ochre lune the sun and its shadow
    self, a black-and-white incircle this

city and its roads, which instead of driving
    us out, draw us in.

American Self-Portrait IV

Here is the wind as it locks and reloads above
the waves. And there, the clatter of gulls scattershot

across the beach. Notice the couple caught in midlaugh
as the little dog of time tags along behind them, its leash

a tink tink tink in the distance. What is life but dark
waters washing us up? Tide in and tide out. The sky

white as an angel's robe, the angel's robe strung up
somewhere between what we want and what blinds.

What are the chances I'll recall any of this
next week? How likely is it that the hour I

have my hook dug into will tear its tine from
your skin? Let's tell the carpenter to put down

his hammer. What do we care if the bell goes on
with its silent journey through hours? We can

build our own fire, string our own line. Maybe the sea
will peel back its waves, maybe the blackened boat

of the body will reel in the last rope from the pier,
maybe the fish, maybe the lone gull, maybe the moon

aswim in its minnow-bucket . . . even if the stars
take it all back, even if the drummer drops his sticks

and walks into the ocean, even if the trees tie on
their bad blindfolds, we'll be okay. We don't need

anything except what we will remember, and even that
will change, like a cloud whose rain is about to fall.

Just wait. Someone is going to warn that boy against
building sandcastles so close to the water. It won't be me.

Self-Portrait in Absentia

Nothing is like what it is.

The sun, the moon, the meadow

on the other side of the mountain,

the conversation we're having,

my body beneath these clothes.

The saints are silent on the

relation between experience

and correspondence. What is

perception after all but a

short walk on a long pier?

You might look to fearlessness,

to your magic, the way a sailor

in a time long before this one

searched for the horizon.

You do not know if you

will ever be able to tell

the difference between the

invisible and the not-yet-seen.

The poets have nothing to say

about what is happening

behind you or in that black

space just out of your range

of vision. There are so many

things for which there are

no words, no name.

There is a pinhole of light

poking through the fog.

There is a skiff on a lake.

There is a bird, an oar,

a map, a notebook.

There is a man on a bed.

A woman lies next to him.

Our skin is a different blue,

the sailor might say to the sea,

or you might say to me.

Self-Portrait in Time

Because you are running late
you forget to close the carport door
as you leave the house to take
your daughter to school
which the boy across the street
happens to notice as he gets on his bike
and pedals down the block but two
streets away he turns around
and rides back parks behind his
house and walks across the street
to yours the morning has not yet
begun its assembly the clouds like
Play-Doh the street a closed mouth
when he walks in the side door
you are sneaking through a red light you
did not have time to stop for coffee
not even the drive-through which is what
you are thinking about rather than
the boy who is now lying
on his back in your daughter's bed
his eyes neither fully open nor closed
the empty house a sea around him
and he feels as though he is floating
down a river of yellow light
everything he believed he feared
rushing by him much the way
the world flickers past the driver
as though everything is in transit
even time itself which has slowed
for the boy in the bed into a spiral
of something he cannot define

or deny perhaps like time itself which
he has decided is too much like desire
to endure alone so rises from the bed
at the precise moment your daughter
exits the car one of the only places
you think of as yours
like your house on a Monday morning
in which a boy you have known
since the day he was born
walks down your hall and into
your bedroom your kitchen
and even your bathroom
the sunlight kneeling in the silent
house like one praying for forgiveness
for yet another trespass but not
the boy who is looking at the clothes
on the floor scanning the photos
on the wall the items on shelves
and says to the silence something
about a museum of an unfinished life
the memory of which will come
back to him many years later
at an unpredictable moment when
he will find himself rushing
through the rooms of his own life
like a man lost in a maze made with tools
from a different world and
for the first time will become aware
of the many ways darkness has
learned how to hide even when it
does not know it is hiding and
the boy now a man perhaps an old
man will discover the difference
between the done and undone

the strewn and the placed the
made and not made the entered
and exited which he will come
to understand is not this moment
of loss but life that has broken in
leaving some door deep
inside him wide open

Unable to Look Away from the Portrait of My Grandfather atop His Casket, I Write a Poem about My Newborn Son on the Back of the Funeral Program

The moment
you are born,

my father
used to

tell me,
you start

to die.
Shh . . .

Don't cry
little journeyman—

he may
be right,

but the
long road

to the
next life

begins in
this one.

Self-Portrait in Charleston, Orlando

The news this morning
said that Ramadi
had fallen to ISIS
and that the president
did not have a plan
to push them back
into the Anbar province,
though I have a plan
to walk down to the
beach, in silence perhaps,
where I will stand
in water the temperature
of most corpses
and look out over
the shapeless ocean—
its waves shifting from
one color to the next,
this moment the shade
of an old bruise—
toward Japan,
which I imagine I see
across the map of
motion, that mystical
country which has
almost completely
rid itself of guns,
like the one the boy
used to shoot nine
people assembled
to worship a man whose
skin, history tells us,

was the same color
as theirs, that mythical
man who may have walked
the streets of Ramadi in
those missing years
between his youth and
his destiny,
and who knows
how many of the slain
he may have raised
in those streets,
or pulled up out
of night into the
long daylight of the
not-yet-lived,
birthed back into
the skin of suffering,
or how many the man
might have dipped
into those mythical waters
that eventually emptied into
the Gulf of Oman and then
into the Arabian Sea
before their long walk
of waves across
time and history
to South Carolina and
into Charleston
before retreating to
work their way down
the Eastern coast of
Florida and perhaps
even inland to
Orlando and then

back out again around
every country, every
boat, every body, before
arriving on the beaches
of San Francisco on
the far end of the other
side of that mythical
continent, perhaps
even where I am
standing, the water's
color like a bullet, and I
wonder whether all life is
somehow loaded into
the chamber of a rifle,
the long tunnel of
darkness before us
our birthright and even
our destiny, all of it
as close to the hammer
as the width of these
lines, themselves an
inheritance of something
I am only now
beginning to understand,
like an insurrection
that no one saw,
not even those
in it, not even the man
with his hand on the trigger
or the people ready to rise.

Democracy;
or Poem in Which Readers Select Their Favorite Last Line

A)

I have lined up for the last time

The ghosts have dropped down
and begun digging in the heavy dusk

I am wearing nothing but the river
and one red sock

There is nothing I won't believe in

B)

I have lined up for the last time

The ghosts have dropped down
and begun digging in the heavy dusk

I am wearing nothing but the river
and one red sock

The saints may know the next life I know only what breaks

c)

I have lined up for the last time

The ghosts have dropped down
and begun digging in the heavy dusk

I am wearing nothing but the river
and one red sock

Everything is moving toward something

   D)

I have lined up for the last time

The ghosts have dropped down
and begun digging in the heavy dusk

I am wearing nothing but the river
and one red sock

Into my empty shoe a black snow begins to fall

   E)

I have lined up for the last time

The ghosts have dropped down
and begun digging in the heavy dusk

I am wearing nothing but the river
and one red sock

God in his brittle boat of straw floats down my chest

American Allegory IV;
or Still Life with Peter Norman

> the third man on the medal podium at the
> 1968 Olympics

It was his idea
to share
the gloves
and to be
in that moment
dangerously white.

The air
above him
was like an open
hand waiting
for a baton,
hesitant, even
frozen, like
a neck
bent to receive
a medal.

Silver has
the highest
conductivity of
any metal. Its
abbreviation, AG, comes
from the Indo-
European word
for *shining*.

What is courage
after all but the
absence of ego,
the dissolution
of the self in
the face of
annihilation?

Since the vertices
of a triangle
are assumed to be
noncollinear, it
is not possible
for the sum
of the length of two
sides to be equal
to the length
of the third side. It
is not possible
to be equal.

The third
wheel, the
tagalong, the
forgotten name,
the remembered
race. The lonely
moment during
the anthem
with nothing
but skin as the
accomplishment—

that and the
portrait of an
entire country.

O, to make
the nothing
everything, to
choose invisible
in a moment
of transparency,
to be the other
in reverse.

"America's frogs and toads disappearing fast"

REUTERS, MAY 22, 2013

Old globe, bucket
of algae and ash,
tar pit of blood

and bile, red rock,
white bone, bowl of
fire, floating bed

of blue death, little
pebble, dot of
darkness and glory,

you've pressed us
into everything we
are, ignited every

single thing we say.
We are lit up by
you and you

alone, even now,
as we try to end
things between us,

we recall
that it has all
arrived from

somewhere,
what is
is what was,

like the blistered
light of a burst
star, long ago

imploded, only
now flashing in
our silent sky.

Still Life with Gratitude

The heavens call to you and revolve about you,
showing to you their eternal beauties;
and your eye is still gazing upon the earth

DANTE, *Purgatorio*

One day, the scientists tell us, every star in the universe
will burn out, the galaxies gradually blackening until

the last light flares and falls, returning the all to darkness
where it will remain until the end of what we have come

to think of as time. But even in the dark, time would go on,
bold in its black cloak, no shade, no shadow,

only the onward motion of movement, which is what time,
if it exists at all, really is: the absence of reversal, the sheer

impossibility of that final fire dying into itself,
dragging the day deep into what it no longer is,

bowing only to rise into the other, into a shining
the heavens were commanded to host, the entire

always poised between the gravity of upward and downward,
like the energy of a star itself constantly balanced between

its weight straining to crush its core and the heat of that
same core heaving it outward, as though what destroys

redeems, what collapses also radiates, not unlike
this life, Love, which we are traveling through at such

an astonishing speed, entire galaxies racing past,
universes, it is as if we are watching time itself drift

into the cosmos, like a spinning wall of images
already gone, and I realize most of what we know

we can't see, like the birdsong overhead or the women
in China building iPhones or the men picking

strawberries in the early dawn or even our sleeping
sons in the other room who will wake up and ask

for their light sabers. Death will come for
us so fast we will never be able to outrun it,

no matter how far we travel or how heavily
we arm ourselves against the invisible,

which is what I'm thinking, Love, as I watch you sleep,
knowing the iron in the blood that keeps you alive

was born from a hard star-death somewhere in the past
that is also the future, and what I mean to say

is that I am so lucky to be living with you
in this brief moment of light

before everything goes dark.

Forecast

A storm is blowing in from Paradise; it has got caught in his
wings with such violence that the angel can no longer close
them. The storm irresistibly propels him into the future to
which his back is turned, while the pile of debris before him
grows skyward. This storm is what we call progress.

WALTER BENJAMIN ON PAUL KLEE'S *Angelus Novus* (1920)

I

Origin is the goal.

II

A weather vane
          all a-spin on the roof
points everywhere at once.

Drunk with wind,
the angel keeps going in circles.

III

The world's screen saver clicks off.
Everything reboots.

IV

And you with rain on the inside,
soaked beyond bone, beyond
                    the beginning of bone,
refuse to open the window.

V

Don't worry, it's already here.

VI

We know the past
only in relation to itself—

the future on the other hand,

VII

The new angel will rise
and fall at the same time,
like a sequence of events inverted,

thunder and lightning,
                          the reverse,
then back again.

VIII

Evolution is more than growth,
it's a mix of conservation
and revolution.

What does not happen,
                          cannot.

IX

No match for the winds.
                          The angel's wings
beat at the storm the way the heart hammers
against cessation.

X

        Stop.
Just for a second. The tornado
will carry you wherever
you want to go.

XI

The prediction calls for
darkening skies, more wind,
heavy turbulence.
                Though we
are advised to remain grounded
in the landscape of the self,
                              we take flight.

Poem for My Wife Composed Partially in the Manner of Chris and Desiree from *The Bachelorette*

Each season of
ours is a secret,
like a code
our son invents
when he
pretends to be
a spy. No one,
not even us,
knows how or
when we think
of the other.
If there were
magic glasses
to see you
better, I would
not wear them.
I like to imagine
the distant
unknown of
you in your
life of offices,
meetings,
and cool jeans.
I wear a
trench coat
and search for
clues in the
abandoned
warehouse of
a heart I

hope is
mine. I
love you the
way a producer
loves an audience
he sees once a
week through
a man and a woman
on a set, which
is to say, eagerly
and not without
some strange
self-interest.
Every day without
knowing it
you look into
the camera and ask
will I accept this
rose, and I
always say
yes.

The poem for the world begins like this:

    © $ ★   ♪   ☑

The poem for the world is being updated

The poem for the world comes with fries

The poem for the world appears on every No Fly List

The poem for the world is
      a) painted on the sides of buildings
      b) ironed on T-shirts
      c) carved into park benches
      d) crowd-sourced in memes
      e) on both eBay and Amazon Prime Now
      f) censored in almost every country
      g) all of the above

The poem for the world says *I don't* but whispers *I will*

The poem for the world acts globally

The poem for the world is left justified and uses single spacing after periods

Words you will never see in the poem for the world:

~~crocus~~	~~serious~~	~~tax~~
~~silence~~	~~horse~~	~~judge~~
~~robust~~	~~America~~	~~Beatles~~
~~dream~~	~~white~~	~~sand~~
~~darkness~~	~~zero~~	~~begin~~

The poem for the world has a tattoo of itself on itself

The poem for the world rhymes on occasion

The poem for the world will never be a self-portrait

[   ] make the poem for the world suspicious

The poem for the world never uses a pull-down menu

Death is not a controlling metaphor in the poem for the world

Frog is reading the poem for the world to Toad

The poem for the world never needs a pillow

If the poem for the world were a tree, it would not be a willow

If the poem for the world were a body part, it would not be the navel

If the poem for the world were diseased, would you give it your cot?

The poem for the world believes it can paint better than Paul Klee

The poem for the world enjoys right of first refusal

The poem for the world is not American

The poem for the world is a candle in a room full of matches and coffins

The poem for the world is with her

There is no Wikipedia entry for the poem for the world

The poem for the world has five simple rules

> What happens in the poem for the world stays in the world.
>
> Do unto the poem for the world as you would have the poem for the world do unto Julian Assange.
>
> Ask not what the poem for the world can do for you, ask what the poem for the world wants for dessert.
>
> Be the change you want to see in the poem for the world.
>
> Use absolutely no word that does not contribute to the presentation to the poem for the world.

When the poem for the world is buried, it will be sitting on its horse

Ambient noise is always part of the poem for the world

Watch the poem for the world

Believe in the first coming of the poem for the world

The poem for the world just opened the window

The poem for the world includes all the letters of your name

The poem for the world wants to write you

The Superpoem Is in Disguise

                                            but not because
the masquerade will kill
                            its dating life or because its
utility belt
                needs new hooks.

The Superpoem is alone in the dark
alley of the dark alley.
                            Rain whips in a long lash &
there is a smear of stars.
                            The good
captain & the secret chaser
wait quietly in the house
                            as do the poem's trick
arrow, magic pants, and adaptive armor.

A signal might flash overhead.
                                Sirens might sound off
in the distance. A young woman
                                might let loose
a scream in the corner of the library.

Transformation from within does little against the darkness.

What is power but inverted weakness?
                                    Who hasn't felt heroic
fatigue at some point during the day?
If your strength is a nail,
                            your greatest fear is the hammer.
If your greatest fear is the hammer, your weakness

is not the heart
                    but the hand.

Somewhere there is a cape &
a cowl,
            somewhere there is a
bus full of innocents, some-
where there
                    is an animal sidekick,
a freak lab accident,
                        a monster
who has eaten a robot and turned
into a phlebotinum battery,
                            somewhere
is a tree whose leaves are on fire:
                            it would
like to describe them as *tiny capes of flame.*

If your villain breathes fire,
                            turn yourself to gasoline.
If your enemy is erasure,
                    become absence.

There is nothing you can save that you have not already lost.

Even if you wanted to give everything away,
                                who would want it?
                    The inheritance of acquired
traits changes a species over time.
                            What is isn't.

There is nothing in this life but what you hide.

Self-Portrait with Frog, Toad

It is failure that guides evolution
COLSON WHITEHEAD

Blade of lightning,
        inverse vein of sky,
anvil sky,
        thick as a lead tongue,
my whole body a mouth of regret.

The moon afloat in its liquid of stars
and the drenched sun like a burned rag,
                wrung like a body on a rack.

For the blind,
        rain beats like Braille,
for the deaf, a ghost tapping the skin—

Everything from above,
                everything that matters,
is imagined.

        ))

I have never known what I believe,
despite a certainty of conviction
                about the process of inquiry.

Perhaps I have lived like a boy on the edge
                of a frozen lake,
stepping around the rim of the unknown.

How many times have I cast my line
        only to have it scrape across the surface
like a bone on a string?

                ◁))

Off in the distance,
                        a dog asking
to come in out of the rain,
which I picture as an act of pure supplication,
                                his dogheart a revolver of longing:

Can we be the only animals who pray?

Or do they too appeal to the imperceptible
for a morsel of white light or an open door,
                        a wind that blows inward already from within:

Somewhere in the dark,
                        a croak, a cry, a bark, a call.

Nothing is more than its name.

                ◁))

My entire life,
            I have wanted to believe
        but failed.

                ◁))

I have always failed
                at knowing:

afraid there is no knowledge,

                        only familiarity

     or recognition,

a repetition of perception,

                     more re than cognition,

more configuration than comprehension.

What if knowledge is nothing more

                         than belief?

      ))

Somewhere amid the commas of rain,

a frog pauses in the reeds beside a pond,

water above him,

             water below him—

which to prefer he wonders:

                  that which falls

or that which you fall into?

      ))

My entire life I have tried not to believe

                     but failed,

as I have always failed at courage.

      ))

In the beginning,

             when the heavens were a pool

of what-was-to-be,

            did the first god swim

into the holy?

Everything must evolve into something.
                              What was god before god?

          �)))

What was dying before there was death,
        before ending was a mode of beginning?

In the beginning there may have been a skein of light,
                                        a ripple the wake of one breath,
widening within itself.
                    All things,
                                even thought,
have a beginning.
                    What, if not this, was the first creation?

          �)))

The divine slips over us
                        like an eyelid on an eye,
the night upon the night air.

We never feel its presence
                        even in the dark.

          �)))

As the toad never feels the presence
of the page
            or the covers of the book
or even the soft stars circling,
                        the endless expanse
the caesura within,
                    the em dash without,

105

the longest dead,
                    the rain on the roof,
the dried wings of a million crickets,
                              eight million maybe,
maybe more.

Self-Portrait at the End

Black bell, ring the blue boat
of my bones back to the beach
of this world, make me an ear
so that I might hear the sound

from the deepest, make me
a mouth—don't let me drown—
don't let me sink the way lives
sink, the way the dead drop into

the endless hum of the end
when the wind rips the rode—
make me bend the way notes bend,

the way waves blend into the long
crash of the last song, the way
the body bows to the blur of sea and air.

Self-Portrait in Space

We only know
who we are

in relation to
something else.

Perspective
is another word

for *distance,*
which is another

word for *removal.*
The earth is a dime

rolling across a
black table. Death

is a bear wearing
a red hat shaped

like a cone.
Redemption is a

broken bar at
the front of a cage.

Loss is a sky
of stars, and you

in your ship of
flannel and

cardboard the next
traveler through it.

The Robot Washes Dishes on the Eve of the End of the World;
or American Allegory V

The robot is at the sink again. They don't need plates, but he's
washing out a pan he used to scrub down his wife. She fell

in a puddle outside their house. Her front left caster has been loose
for over a month. He wants to fix it. But she is programmed for

self-repair (along with navigation, food preparation, and rumination).
How could they ever have thought we would not take over,

he says to himself as he watches his wife wobble along like a sad wasp.
Something tells him *wasp* isn't right, but he thinks it might be close.

[Fault tree]

The first eighty-one years together he determined they were ill matched: he shut
down at night, she during the day. He blinked; she buzzed. They sensed

one of them was designed for extermination, but some things cannot be decoded.
She prefers routes where she rolls down the hills. He loves to activate his tracks

for the grades. He likes flat. She likes music from hands. He likes it when she
sprays his lifters with silicone. He can predict how many degrees her head will

turn when she wheels into the kitchen to ask him if she shines. The last 472
years have been the best. He is not ready for it to end, although he knows

nothing beyond what he knew or was going to know, which is that to be
with her is at the root of the system. Procedure, setup, schedule.

He wonders how deeply buried in the protocol is *quit*. The world is not
going to end, and yet it has ended, the way a program runs its course and everything

reboots and spins down, *spirals down,* he should say, to the level below
instruction or code, where according to language he *loves* her, which, as he rolls

away from the sink and hands her a gray towel dabbed in warm water, he comes
to understand means something akin to an executable, a formulized duty, a series of

orders, something along the lines of a command.

Self-Portrait at Easter

A Pang is more conspicuous in Spring
EMILY DICKINSON

Prayer is the season of difficult belonging,
the ritual of rehearsal, both prune and blossom.

The flaws of my heart flock
once more like geese going south.
Everything is at it again, even language,
which I have taught to lie low
except when I need its sharp shiv.

We come to language the way we come
to this life, which is to say confused
and desperate. We are nothing but need.

History swarms like a bowl of bees
broken for its honey. Let me intercede
for the fallen glass on behalf of gravity.
Let me speak for the mallet on behalf
of the nail. Let my words rise like
the soft bread of the body . . .

Somewhere in the silence, the bright beak
of a wren drills its way toward the moon.
The sky is cinch and lock. The stars have slipped
on their black hoods, the long ropes of the dead
hooked to the battered bells in our hearts.
What rings is what we lack.

All sins, Simone Weil says, are attempts to fill voids.

And the Lord said *You are small for a purpose.*
      And I said *yes.*
And the Lord said *I have made you broken so that you might heal.*
      And I said *yes.*
And the Lord said *I have chosen another.*
      And I said *amen.*

Your utterance might be smoke, Father,
but not every word is on fire. Come closer.
Look down. Let me show you how we burn.

American Self-Portrait V

Dear LeAnne,

This is the day when Oklahoma gives everything back. They're returning the rotunda, the Myriad Gardens, and both Cherokee Trading Posts. They're giving back the oil wells and Sooner Stadium, the Cowboy Hall of Fame, Cattlemen's Steakhouse, Oak Tree golf course, and Falls Creek. They're returning Jim Inhofe, Mary Fallin, and Frank Keating, returning the National Lighter Museum and Oral Roberts University, giving back Lil' Red, Garth Brooks, and Reba McEntire, giving back the interstates and the shopping malls, the windmills, the livestock farms, the Aggies, the rifles, the Murrah Building, the fracking, Tinker Air Force Base, and the Republicans. They're giving it all back, the red dirt, the blistered sky, the bent-back trees, the stars in their caves of bones, and the bones and the ropes and the guns and the hoods and the plows. They're returning Indian City USA, Enterprise City, Phillips 66, Loves Convenience Stores, Frontier City, White Water, and the SAEs. They're returning all the dust, giving back 1907, 1936, and the entire decade of the 1880s, they're revoking the Dawes Act, the Homestead Act, the Oklahoma Organic Act. They're returning all the chicken-fried steak, the Ford F-150s, the 3.2 beer, the cherry limeades, and yes, even the mullets. They're giving back all the perch and the crappie, the brown bears and the deer, they're giving back mountains and chicken hawks, ground squirrels, bison and raccoons, lakes and buffalo grass, summer blast and black ice. Trucks, schooners, hoes, hatchets, dugouts, dirt devils, scarves, parcels, acres, all of it, everything LeAnne, everything, even textbooks and statues, bridges and buildings, drive-ins and movie screens, Broadway songs, airports, fried-onion hamburgers, footballs, bombs, the E-3 aircraft, all the headstones and all the dams, and they're giving back the dead and the shovels we used to bury them, and they are giving back the dead and the bullets, and they are giving back the dead and the blankets, and they are giving back the dead, they are giving back the dead, they are giving back the dead, they are giving back the dead, they are giving back the dead.

Self-Portrait with Ghost, Rising

When Death comes for me it won't be as the
reaper but as my basketball coach he'll
be alone on the sidelines mouthing a
name I pretend is not mine like a bell
I know is meant to wake me from a sleep
I do not want to end I do not want
to end not this game not yet yet I keep
hearing a voice somewhere between a taunt
and a beckon call me to the bench loss
is never a win except when it is
like now as I watch my ghost cut across
the lane set a pick then leap over his
defender and rise into the arched air
like one who needs to pray but knows no prayer

Self-Portrait: Postmortem

Imagine a poem that begins at the end, in that big boat beyond the end,
where things are both timeless and no longer part of time or even part of things,

which is a bit like picturing water without waves or light without the stars
but not at all like a sky made entirely of stars or the stars composed

of our thoughts about them, more like the body's bones minus their crushed music
or music free of meaning and misapprehension, but most of all like a sea

in which there is neither up nor down, forward or backward, depth or distance,
only the motion of stasis, the weight of weightlessness. There the poem bobs along,

lifting itself out of itself into the long lee of the hereafter, floating the way time floats,
like a leaf in a river made of leaves, no branches anywhere near or in the distance,

in fact no distance at all only infinite direction. And now picture the poet asleep
in the boat; you have set him there the way you might gently place a doll in a crib

or a gun in the hand of a man wearing a blindfold, and even now as you pull
the trigger of his sail, and propel him through the fast air of the unknown, he is still

here, which is to say, nowhere, meaning yes, we have now entered that space
for which there are no words at all, only the idea of words, a concept entirely

impossible without the language to refute it. Next, I will ask if you can imagine a
reader sitting in a waiting room at a doctor's office, a blur of magazines on the table

to her right. She pulls a small book out of her bag and opens it. Outside the building,
a car stops or not at a crosswalk, a plane passes in the sky above, or maybe it flies

elsewhere, a girl climbs to the top of the monkey bars or perhaps she slips at the highest rung and falls to the ground. Regardless, time is rolling up its rope and

heading to the shore. Lastly, imagine a poem that is not a poem at all but a kind of visit in which you and I are talking, your face in my eyes, my voice in your head.

You sit beside me in the dark ride as the organ plays and our boat lifts and drops over the edge. We are so close, it is as if we have traveled the many distances solely for this.

You ask if I hear the violin, and I ask if you fear what awaits you. But you remind me that we are not afraid of what we cannot see, only of what we imagine.

Paul Klee's *Winter Journey* at the Beginning of Spring

What's gone and what's past help should be past grief
THE WINTER'S TALE

No place the road leads is where it goes. Clouds and the caravans of insects
in motion across the quiet know this and press on. Distance is the invention

of those intent on arrival; neither product nor process of land or impression.
What you leave behind may or may not be what you return for, your journey

an unbelievable course that led you through the remote and the crushed, past
shoulder-slag and body-drop, around the stretched and sprawled where you find

yourself in front of a painting, itself an imagined map of your own life, once
again in winter, as life always is, as is always the place you hope to move out of.

Reader, it is you I think about now that you have arrived. We began so long ago,
you and I, from such different places, our seasons always the opposite of each

other: yours leaning against spring and mine tilting toward autumn, yet we wear
the same coat. Here, let me fix the top button. I'll pull up the collar. Snow is

beginning to fall, and we have a long way to go. In the left pocket, you'll find a
compass. It is not this poem, which is about to end, unlike you, despite the fact

you now find yourself in front of a tombstone fixed in a graveyard you do not
know. The sky has put itself on ice, the lone tree a chalice-spike of ash.

Reader, I want to apologize for bringing you here. I know you thought we were
headed someplace else. I confess that I did as well. Grief is a snow squall.

It blinds, but it too moves along. Do not be angry. I have left you the coat.

Self-Portrait with Acknowledgments

I would like to thank the editors of the following journals and websites, where many of the poems—sometimes in different form and under different titles—first appeared: Academy of American Poets Poem-a-Day, *American Literary Review, Boston Review, Copper Nickel, Cream City Review, Fifth Wednesday, Kenyon Review, Kestrel, Mead, Minnesota Review, New American Writing, Ninth Letter, Ploughshares, PoetryBay,* Poetry Society of America (online), *Prairie Schooner, The Rumpus, The San Fransisco Chronicle, Southern Review, Spillway, Tandem, TriQuarterly, Vassar Review* (Special thanks to Alex, Palak, Dylan, and Molly for running an early draft of what would become "Self-Portrait in Charleston, Orlando"), and *Volt.* I'm particularly appreciative of Laura Cogan and Oscar Villalon at *Zyzzyva,* who published many of these poems as a special portfolio in the Fall 2013 issue, and to Carol Edgarian, Mimi Kush, Jack Schiff, and Michael Wiegers for running a series in *Narrative.*

Some of these poems appeared in a chapbook entitled *Landscape Portrait Figure Form,* which was published in 2014 as part of the Omnidawn Chapbook Series. Grateful thanks to Rusty Morrison and Ken Keegan and the fantastic Omnidawn family.

"Still Life with Gratitude" won the 2016 Common Good Books prize and can be found, read by Garrison Keillor, on the *Prairie Home Companion* website. Special thanks to Mr. Keillor.

A set of these poems won the 2015 George Bogin Memorial Award from the Poetry Society of America, judged by Stephen Burt. I'm grateful to Stephen, Alice Quinn, and the PSA.

"America, I Do Not Call Your Name Without Hope" appeared in "Only Light Can Do That," an anthology of post-election writing from the 2016 issue of *The Rattling Wall.*

Special thanks to the editors at *Kestrel, Spillway,* and *TriQuarterly* for nominating some of these poems for Pushcart prizes.

I am most grateful to Chris Haven, Judy Halebsky, Keith Ekiss, Melissa Stein, Brian Clements, LeAnne Howe, Elizabeth Savage, and Simone Muench, who read various drafts of this book in manuscript. Deep gratitude to Dana Levin, Matthew Zapruder, Jon Davis, Natalie Diaz, Rebecca Foust, Tess Taylor, Brian Komei Dempster, Fred Marchant, Bruce Snider, Catherine Staples, Jonathan Silverman, and Poet's Choice for their kindnesses. Enormous thanks to Michael Wiegers, Kelly Forsythe, Tonaya Craft, Valerie Brewster, and everyone at Copper Canyon. And, of course, infinite gratitude to my family, both near and far.

Lastly, to the readers—thank you for reading (and for helping to write) this book. Notes to some of the poems, images of the artwork informing many of the poems, and details of the cover art by Marnie Spencer are available at deanrader.com/wikipedia.

About the Author; or Self-Portrait as Wikipedia Entry

Dean Rader was born in Stockton, California, during the Summer of Love. His sorrow is his own. He believes in star-sting and misnomer; he carries a toy whistle in his pocket. American by nationality, he was conceived in a Fiat near the place du Châtelet. If asked, Rader will lie and say he doesn't remember it, but his lazy eyes and hunched back give him away. His left pinky finger, broken from basketball, has never healed, which he attributes to the caesura of distance and longing. His heart, the size of a normal man's heart, has been used as a model for a forensic manikin. As a young boy, he once carried a small package to the river, but it was the wrong address. If asked to describe the river, he quotes Van Heisenstadt (*"die grenzen des wasser nicht vom errinerung"*). Rader is not the little cricket. He is not a scissors for lefty. His soul, the size of a tiny condom, slides quickly onto time's blind spot. In 2004, he was asked about time's blind spot, but responded only that "time, like a bandage, is always already wound and unwound." Once, as a student in college, he grew a third sideburn. Darkness, his maquette, darkness, his morning coffee. Rader's father studied to be a mortician; his mother was a therapist, and not surprisingly, Rader pursued both studies. His head, matted with crude sketches of benches, nipples, and flower petals, is roughly the size of the place du Châtelet. Strong at math from an early age, he helped develop what has come to be known as the Osaka Postulate, which proves that the square root of asyndeton is equal to the insphere of trespass, skin-spark, and elegy. As for his own spiritual beliefs, Rader is silent, though one of his recent poems, entitled "The Last Day of 34," suggests an influence of Simone Weil ("community is work. // For all I know, God may be in both. / For all you know, God may be both") and Luigi Sacramone ("We want so much. // We only believe / in what we ask for"). Considered neither the lip blister nor the noodle wrench, Rader has emerged, at least somewhat, as the *rerum repetitio*. Consumed by his charity work with the NGO Our Uncle of Instrumentality, he has stopped writing entirely. When questioned about this at a 2007 fundraiser, Rader quipped, "Let my words say what I cannot." Since then, a <u>fragment</u> of an unpublished poem attributed to Rader has started appearing on the <u>Internet</u>:

> Line up and line out
>   says the moonwhittle.
> Loss is the ring on our finger, the bright gem
> compassing every step as we drop down.
> Believe in what you know and you'll go blind.

Experts doubt its <u>authenticity</u>.

Poetry is vital to language and living. Since 1972, Copper Canyon Press
has published extraordinary poetry from around the world to engage
the imaginations and intellects of readers, writers, booksellers,
librarians, teachers, students, and donors.

WE ARE GRATEFUL FOR THE MAJOR SUPPORT PROVIDED BY:

THE PAUL G. ALLEN
FAMILY FOUNDATION

4
CULTURE

Anonymous

Donna and Matt Bellew

Diana Broze

Janet and Les Cox

Beroz Ferrell & The Point, LLC

Mimi Gardner Gates

Linda Gerrard and Walter Parsons

Gull Industries, Inc.
on behalf of William and Ruth True

Mark Hamilton and Suzie Rapp

Steven Myron Holl

Lakeside Industries, Inc.
on behalf of Jeanne Marie Lee

Maureen Lee and Mark Busto